FELLA ALWAYS SA

LOVE THAT'S NOT

MA USETA MAKE WHEN YOU WERE A LI

FOR WHEN YOU GO ON THE BATTER WIT

IRISH SLANG THAT MAKES A HOLY SHOV

TS FOR GOBDAWS AS THICK AS MANURE

ISH SLANG THAT'S GREAT CRAIC FOR

QUOTATIONS SOME SMART FECKER IN

K OF IRISH SONGS YER OUL' FELLA ALW

CKIN' BOOK OF IRISH SEX & LOVE THAT'S

UVELY IRISH RECIPES YER MA USETA M

BOOK OF IRISH SAYINGS FOR WHEN YOU

E 2ND FECKIN' BOOK OF IRISH SLANG T

KIN' BOOK OF IRISH INSULTS FOR GOBD

THE BOOK OF FECKIN' IRISH SLANG TH

BOOK OF DEADLY IRISH QUOTATIONS S

' ON ABOUT THE BOOK OF IRISH SONGS

AT A HOOLEY THE FECKIN' BOOK OF I

S EYES THE BOOK OF LUVELY IRISH REC

URRIER THE FECKIN' BOOK OF IRISH SAY

VER OF SAVAGES THE 2ND FECKIN' BOO

IE FIRST ONE THE FECKIN' BOOK OF I

AND ONLY HALF AS USEFUL THE BOO

W9-AUB-977

The book of feckin' Irish Slang that's great craic for cute hoors and bowsies

The Feckin' Collection

ARE YOU ACTIN' THE MAGGIOT, YE MANKY WAGON?
GO AND ASK ME ARSE, YE GANKY MUCK SAVAGE.

The book of feckin' Irish Slang that's great craic for cute hoors and bowsies

Colin Murphy & Donal O'Dea

THE O'BRIEN PRESS
DUBLIN

First published 2004 by The O'Brien Press Ltd,
12 Terenure Road East, Rathgar, Dublin 6, Ireland.
Tel: +353 1 4923333; Fax: +353 1 4922777
E-mail: books@obrien.ie Website: www.obrien.ie
Reprinted 2004 (three times), 2005, 2006, 2007, 2008, 2009.

ISBN: 978-0-086278-829-2

Copyright for text, illustrations and design
© Colin Murphy/Donal O'Dea 2004

All rights reserved. No part of this publication may be reproduced or utilised in any form or by any means, electronic or mechanical, including photocopying, recording or in any information storage and retrieval system, without permission in writing from the publisher.

British Library Cataloguing-in-Publication Data
Murphy, Colin
The book of feckin' Irish slang that's great craic for cute hoors and bowsies. - (Feckin' collection ; bk.2)
1. English language - Ireland - Slang
I.Title II.O'Dea, Donal
427.9'415

9 10 11 12
09 10 11 12

Printed and bound by Scandbook AB, Sweden.

What's the story?

'Did you hear that the scrubber and the wagon were plastered last night and ended up in a mill? It was deadly!'

This sentence makes perfect sense to most Irish people. But to everyone else on the planet it means the following:

'Did you hear that the cleaning utensil and the four wheeled horse-drawn vehicle were covered in a lime/sand/water mixture and then transported to a processing factory, with fatal consequences.'

This book sets out to avoid any such confusion arising in the future by explaining in clear and precise terms the meaning of a vast number of commonly used Irish slang words or expressions. If you, dear reader, believe that any of the listed phrases have been incorrectly translated, please feel free to go and ask my arse.

Acting the Maggot (expression)

Fooling about in a somewhat boisterous manner.
(usage) 'Anto! Will you stop acting de maggot and give the oul' wan back her wheelchair.'

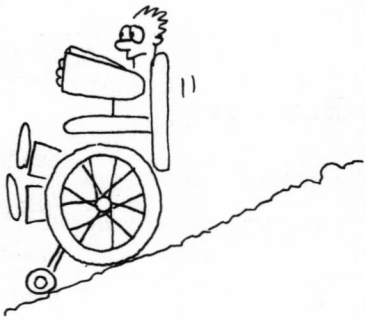

Arseways (adj)

Mishmash. Complete disarray. Total mess.
(usage) 'Me car has been arseways since I ran over the pedestrian.'

Ask me arse (v)(rhetorical)

What do you take me for, a silly billy?
(usage) 'Lend YOU a fiver? Go and ask me arse!'

Bad dose (n)

Severe illness.
(usage) 'I'd a bad dose of the scutters after them ten pints of Guinness last night.'

Bags (n)

(see *also* Hames)

A botched job.
(usage) 'The hairdresser made a right bags of me perm.'

Bang on (adj)

Correct. Perfectly accurate.
(usage) 'That shot ye took at the ref's groin was bang on.'

Banjaxed (adj)

(see also Knackered)

Broken. Severely damaged.
(usage) 'Me marriage to Deco is completely banjaxed.'

Barrel (v)

Hurry. Race. Rush.
(usage) 'When the Guards arrived, the Minister for Justice barrelled out of the Lap Dancing Club.'

BIFFO

(acronym)

Big Ignorant Fucker From Offaly.
(usage) 'Em, excuse me BIFFO, would you mind not using the table cloth as a hanky?'

Black Stuff (n)

Stout.
(usage) 'Nine pints of the black stuff and a gin and tonic for de mot please.'

Blarney (n)

Nonsense talk used to charm foreigners. *(eg) 'They say the ghost of Finn Mac Cumhall still stalks the Grand Canal. Buy another round and I'll tell you all about it, my American friend.'*

Blather (n) (v)

Empty, worthless talk. *(usage) 'What are ye blatherin' on about, Taoiseach?'*

Bogtrotter (n)

(*see also* BIFFO, Culchie, Mucksavage, Mulchie)

A person of rural extraction. *(usage) 'And that, my bogtrotter friend, is what we call electricity.'*

Bollixed (adj)

(*see also* Fluthered, Gee-eyed, Langered, Ossified, Paralytic, Plastered, Rat-arsed)

Somewhat in excess of the legal alcohol driving limit.
(usage) 'After twelve pints I was a bit bollixed.'

Bowsie (n)

Person (esp. male) of very disreputable character. A useless good-for-nothing.
(usage) 'Is there anyone in the Government who isn't a bleedin' bowsie?'

Boyo (n)

Male juvenile (esp. delinquent). *(usage) 'Y'know sarge, I think dem boyos outside the off-licence are up to no good with dem crowbars and flick-knives.'*

Brasser (n)

A lady of the night. *(usage) 'As a judge, it's my job to keep brassers like you off the street. So get into the bloody car!'*

Brutal **(adj)**

Awful, terrible, hideous.
(usage) 'The head on her was brutal.'

Bucketing down **(v)**

Raining cats and dogs.
(usage) 'Sure it's bucketing down outside. Might as well have another six pints.'

Caught rapid **(expression)**

Caught in the act. Proven guilty beyond doubt.
(usage) 'I was caught rapid in bed with me mistress by me bit on the side.'

Chiseller (n)

Young child.
(usage) 'That slapper's only eighteen and she's already had three chisellers.'

Clatter (v)(n)

To slap playfully with palm.
(usage) 'I only gave him one little clatter, yer Honour. His skull musta been brittle.'

Cod (v)

(see *also* Let on)

To pull one's leg in a jovial fashion.
(usage) 'Ah, sure I was only coddin'. Your wife wasn't electrocuted at all.'

Craic (n)

(Pronounced crack)

Fun.

(usage) 'There's great craic to be found in that pub on the corner.' (Note: Misinterpretation of this expression has led to several arrests of foreign visitors who were caught trying to purchase a particular illicit drug.)

Culchie (n)

(see also BIFFO, Bogtrotter, Mucksavage, Mulchie)

A person whose birthplace is beyond Dublin city limits.

(usage) Q: 'What d'ye call a culchie in a stretch Limo?'
A: 'The deceased.'

Cute hoor (n)

Suspiciously resourceful gentleman.
(usage) 'Speaking from his yacht off Bermuda, the cute hoor denied he'd made any payments to politicians in return for favourable building contracts.'

Deadly (adj)

Great, brilliant, fantastic.
'Yer woman's got a deadly arse.'

Dense (adj)

Stupid. Thick.
(usage) 'My accountant and solicitor say that paying tax is dense.'

Desperate (adj)

(Pronounced despera) Dreadful, awful.
'Yer man's arse is desperate after a few pints.'

Diddies (n)

Extremely childish term for a woman's breasts.
(usage) 'Counsel for the defence has got a magnificent pair of diddies, hasn't she m'Lud?'

Donkey's Years (n)

Inordinately long time. An epoch. Time immemorial.

(eg) Period of time people of Ireland have been waiting for a National Soccer Stadium.

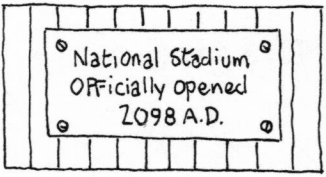

Doss (on the) (n)

Failure to attend school/work during specified hours.

'I swear I wasn't on de doss. I really did have leukaemia yesterday.'

Dosser (n)

Person with a relaxed attitude to attendance at his/her place of employment.
(eg) Dosser: 'Hey Mick, will ye move dis piano for me while I go an get me medicine in dat chemist, beside dat pub?'

Drawers (n)

Knickers. Panties.
(usage) 'You could fit a hurling team into me wife's drawers. In fact I think she does on a regular basis.'

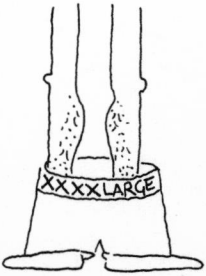

Dry Shite (n)

Someone of limited verbal/social skills. *(usage) 'There was a dry shite on the seat beside me at the client party.'*

Eat the head off (v)

To rebuke verbally in an aggressive manner. *(usage) 'The missus ate de head off me just because I puked into de back of the TV.'*

Eccer (n)

Homework *(usage) 'Hey, Ma. Do me eccer for me or I'll tell Da about the postman.'*

Eejit (n)

Person of limited mental capacity. Incapable fool. Complete moron. Imbecile.

(eg) Person(s) responsible for Ireland's health service.

Effin' and blindin' (expression)

Swearing profusely.

(usage) 'The Taoiseach was effin' and blindin' because the new Government jet didn't have the Playboy Channel.'

Eff off (v)

Restrained/polite swear word used in refined Irish society. *(usage) 'Father, those chappies on the factory floor told me to 'eff off' when I inquired if they'd made my morning tea.'*

Fair play! (expression)

Well done! *(usage) 'Fair play te ye for gettin' de leg over Deirdre.'*

Fanny (n)

Female genitals.

(usage) 'That Deirdre's fanny was as tight as camel's hole in a sand-storm.'

(Warning: Some American visitors have inadvertently caused shock or offence through the mistaken belief that 'fanny' refers to buttocks, as it does in the US. eg 'After that bike ride, I feel like giving my fanny a good rub,' may raise some eyebrows if spoken aloud in public.)

Feck (v)(n)

Politically correct term for f**k.

(usage) 'Ah feck off Father Murphy. You're nothing but a feckin' fecker.'

Fierce (adj)

Very. Extremely.
(usage) 'I had a fierce bad headache after drinking Deirdre's perfume.'

Fine Thing (n)

(*see also* Ride)

An attractive man or woman.
(usage) 'She looks like a fine thing after seven pints.'

Flahulach (adj)

(Pronounced Flah-hule-uck)

Generous.
(usage) 'The councillor was feeling flahulach after he got his bribe from the property developer.'

Fluthered (adj)

(see *also* Bollixed, Gee-eyed, Langered, Ossified, Paralytic, Plastered, Rat-arsed.)

Having a high blood/alcohol ratio. *(usage) 'I was so fluthered last night I slept with the missus.'*

Fooster (v)

Not getting much done. Fiddling about. *(usage) 'Will ye stop foosterin' about Mick and stamp on the goalie's face!'*

Full shilling (adj)

(not the)

Mentally challenged. Not fully sane. Nuts. *(eg) Anyone who attempts to commute by means of public transport in Dublin or Cork on a regular basis is said to be 'not the full shilling'.*

Gaa (n)

Sport played by the G.A.A. (Gaelic Athletic Association). *(usage) 'Gaa is a great game. It's just a shame about the G.A.A.'*

Gaff (n)

Home. Place of residence.
(usage) 'Dat's some gaff yer woman de President has in de Phoenix Park.

Gammy (adj)

Damaged. Crooked. Useless.
(usage) 'The entire Cabinet is gammy.'

Gander (n)

A quick glance.
(usage) 'I'd give anything for a gander at Noleen in the nip.'

Ganky (adj)

Repulsive. Ugly.
(usage) Q. What's the difference between a ganky-looking girl and an absolute ride?
A. About ten pints!

Gansey-load (adj)

Many. Lots. An excess.
(usage) 'There's a gansey-load of dossers in the Dáil.'

Gargle (n) (v)

Drink (alcohol)
(usage) The Cabinet single-handedly prevented the closure of the brewery by retiring to the Dáil bar for a 'gargle or two'.

Gas (adj)

Amusing. Funny. Hilarious.
(usage) 'It was gas when Cormac broke his collar-bone.'

Gawk (v)

To stare rudely.
(usage) 'What are you gawking at ye ignorant gobshite?'

Gee (n)

Female reproductive organ.
(usage) 'I've a pain in me gee trying to get laid tonight.'

Geebag (n)

Woman of unpleasant character.
(usage) 'Me wife's a right geebag.'

Gee-Eyed (adj)

(see also Bollixed, Langered, Ossified Paralytic, Plastered, Rat-arsed)

Having partaken of large quantity of ales/ spirits.
(orig) *Subject was so inebriated that his eyes have shifted from the normal horizontal orientation.*

Get off with (v)

Be successful with a romantic advance.
(usage) 'I got off with four different fellas at the Christmas party.'

Go and shite!

(expression)
(*see also* Ask me Arse, Get up the Yard)

I am not in agreement with your suggestion.
(usage) 'The priest told me to abstain from bad language, so I told him to go and shite!'

Gobdaw (n)

(see *also* Gobshite)

Person of restricted mental ability.
(usage) 'The Minister for Finance is a complete gobdaw.'

Gobshite (n)

(see *also* Gobdaw)

Person of below average IQ. Socially inept individual.
(usage) 'The Minister for Finance is a complete gobshite.'

Gollier (n)

A mass of phlegm expelled from mouth at high speed.
(usage) 'I landed a gollier in the geography teacher's coffee.'

Gombeen man (n)

Petty, snivelling, fawning underling.
(eg) Chief executive of any Irish semi-state company.

Gouger (n)

Aggressive, repulsive person.
(usage) 'Do you really take this gouger to be your lawful wedded husband?'

Guff (n)

Feeble excuses.
Blatant lies.
(eg) 'Sorry I'm late, boss. I had to take me Ma to the hospital for her spine replacement operation.'

Gurrier (n)

Hooligan. Delinquent. Ruffian.

(usage) 'Give the oul' lad back his teeth, ye little gurrier!'

Hames (n)

Complete mess.

(usage) 'The plastic surgeon made a hames of me arse.'

Head-the-ball (n)

Term of address: 'you'.

(usage) 'Hey, head-the-ball, how do I get to Donegal?'

Heavin' (adj):

Thoroughly packed.
(usage) 'In the planning trial the defendant's box was heavin' with County Councillors.'

Hockeyed (v)

Heavily defeated.
(usage) 'Ireland hockeyed Brazil five-nil in the World Cup Final, and then me bleedin' missus woke me up.'

Hole (n)

Anus.
(usage) 'Piles are a pain in the hole.'

Holy Joe (n)

Self-righteous, sanctimonious hypocrite.

(usage) If Holy Joes a so holy, how come there's always so mar of them queuing for confession?

Holy show (expression)

Disgrace. Spectacle.

(usage) 'Me Ma mad a holy show of herself when she dropped he pint into the baptism font.'

Hooley (n)

Raucous celebration involving drinking and singing.

(usage) ' ... and folks, I'm asked to invite you all to a hooley in Murphy's pub immediately after Mick's funeral.'

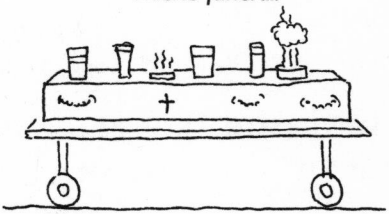

Hop (v)

Play truant from school.

(usage) 'Let's go on the hop and get pissed. I'm fed up teaching those bleedin' kids anyway.'

Howaya **(greeting)**

Hello. Hi.

(usage) 'Howaya, ye big bollix!'

How's she cuttin'? **(expression)** How is life, my good friend?

(usage) 'How's she cuttin', yer honour?'

How's the craic? **(expression)**

How are you? What's happening?

(usage) 'How's the craic, Deirdre?'

I will in me arse/ bollix/hole/fanny (expression)

I absolutely refuse to do what you suggest. *(usage) 'Marry you? I will in me bollix!'*

Jackeen (n)

A rural person's derogatory name for a Dubliner. *(usage) Q: 'What does a Jackeen say on his first day in work?' A: 'What do I do now, Daddy?'*

Jacks (n)

Toilet, restroom.

(usage) 'Ye tink dat's bad? Wait 'til ye see de state of de jacks in de Dáil.'

Jammers (adj)

Extremely crowded.

(usage) 'The Dáil bar is permanently jammers.'

Jammy (adj)

Exceedingly lucky.
(usage) 'The jammy bastard won the Lotto again.'

Janey Mack! (expression)

Expression of utter disbelief. Wow!
(usage) 'Janey Mack! That politician told the truth!'

Jar (n)

Pint of beer or stout.
(usage) 'I'm dying for a jar. The court will adjourn until 2pm.'

Jaysus! (expression)

Jesus Christ!
(usage) 'Ah Jaysus, ye puked in me pint!'

Jo Maxi (n)

Taxi. Cab.
(usage) 'Eh hello. I'd like a Jo Maxi please to collect four people from Madame Le Whip's Maison de Plaisir *and take us back to Government Buildings.*

Joe Soap (n)

Anybody. Somebody. Nondescript person.
(usage) 'I shagged some Joe Soap last night.'

Kick the shite out of (v)

Violently assault, causing actual bodily harm.
(usage) 'Right lads, we're down 2-0. Let's kick the shite out of dem.'

Kip (n)

A place/establishment of poor repute.
A dump.
(usage) 'Benidorm is a kip.'

Knackered (adj)

(see *also* Banjaxed)

Very tired. Broken beyond repair.
(usage) 'My arse was banjaxed after that vindaloo.'

Knockers (n)

Mammaries. Breasts.

(usage) 'Are dem knockers real, missus?'

Langer (n)

Male reproductive organ.

(usage)

Countrywoman A: 'This carrot reminds me of me husband's langer.'

Countrywoman B: 'Ye mean the size of it?'

Countrywoman A: 'No. The dirt of it.'

Langered (adj)

(*see also* Bollixed, Ossified, Paralytic, Fluthered, Gee-eyed, Plastered, Rat-arsed)

Very drunk.
(usage) 'I was so langered I woke up with a kebab in me knickers.'

Lash (v)

To rain heavily.
(usage) 'We had two weeks' holiday in the sunny south-east and it never stopped bleedin' lashin'.'

Leg it (v)

To flee rapidly. To run away.
(usage) 'Let's leg it before the waiter comes back with the bill, Sarge.'

Loaf (v)

To head-butt.
(usage) 'Righ', Murphy. As a bouncer, your primary job is to loaf everyone who tries to get into this bleedin' nightclub.'

Manky (adj)

Disgustingly filthy.
(eg) Any street, waterway, public toilet, or beauty spot in Ireland.

Massive (adj)

Great. Fantastic.
(usage) 'Look at the tiny little arse on yer woman. It's massive!'

Mentaller (n)

Nut case. Looney.
(usage) Politician: 'Commissioner, about 1000 of the Gardai are complete mentallers!" Commissioner: 'I know, it's just not enough, is it?'

Me oul' segotia

(expression)

Term of endearment.
My old flower.
(usage) 'Any chance of a ride, me oul' segotia?'

Mill (n)(v)

Fight. Public brawl.
(usage) 'Hey, look lads! A mill between wimmin'!'

Mitch (v)

(see *also* Hop)

To play truant. To skip school.

(usage) 'Honest, we're not mitchin', Guard. We're doin' a project on juvenile alcohol consumption.'

Mortified (adj)

(see *also* Scarlet)

Highly embarrassed.

(usage) 'I was mortified when the baby came out black.'

Mot (n)

Girlfriend.

(usage) 'Me mot drinks tequila sunrises like there's no tomorrow.'

Muck savage (n)

(*see also* BIFFO, Culchie, Mulchie)

Country fellow lacking in sophistication.
(usage) 'No, you big muck savage, you may not eat curry chips in the delivery room.'

Mulchie (n)

(*see also* BIFFO, Culchie, Muck savage.)

Person from a small rural town.
(usage) 'That, my mulchie friend, is a three-storey building.'

Murder (adj)

Very difficult. Almost impossible.
(usage) 'Getting a Cavan man to buy his round is murder.'

Nip (in the) (adj)

Nude. Naked.
(usage) 'The doctor examined me in the nip. Whatever happened to his clothes is anyone's guess.'

Nixer (n)

Job done on the side, for cash, thus avoiding tax. *(usage) 'Tell you what, I'll write your next Budget speech as a nixer, Minister.'*

Oul' wan (n)

Mother.
(usage) 'Me oul' wan had me when she was sixteen.'

Oul' fella (n)

Father.
(usage) 'Me oul' fella hasn't been seen since.'

Oirish (n)

Mythical language and culture used by Americans and British when portraying Irish people.
(eg) 'Top of de mornin' te ye, be de hokey. D'ye happen te know, me good sir, where I'd be findin' a leprechaun dis fine day, at all at all?'

Ossified (adj)

(see *also* Bollixed Fluthered, Gee-eyed, Langered Paralytic, Rat-arsed.)

Totally inebriated.
(usage) 'Do you know it takes just three pints to get an Englishman ossified?'

THREE PINTS OF GUINNESS AND A SICK BUCKET FOR MY ENGLISH FRIEND.

Paralytic (adj)

(*see also* Bollixed Fluthered, Gee-eyed, Langered, Ossified, Plastered, Rat-arsed.)

So inebriated one actually passes out. *(usage) 'Do you know that it takes just four pints to get an Englishman paralytic?'*

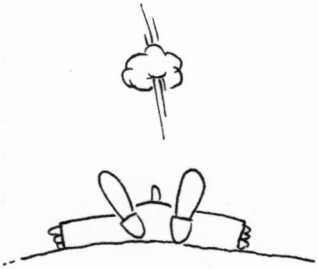

Piss up (n)

Night of revelry and imbibing alcohol. *(usage) 'I must interrupt counsel's lengthy summation to remind him that the barristers' annual piss-up starts at five.'*

Plastered (adj)

(see *also* Bollixed, Fluthered, Gee-eyed, Langered, Ossified, Paralytic, Rat-arsed.)

Very drunk.
(usage) 'I was so plastered that the taxi-driver actually made sense.'

Puss (n)

Sulky face.
(usage) 'Frank had a puss on him just because me and the girls were watching Emmerdale during the World Cup Final.'

Rapid (adj)

Great. Fantastic. Amazing.
(usage) 'Yer mot's knockers are rapid.'

Rat-arsed (adj)

(*see also* Bollixed, Fluthered, Gee-eyed, Langered, Ossified, Paralytic, Rat-arsed)

Very drunk.
(usage) 'I was so rat-arsed I ate a spiceburger.'

Reddner (n)

Blush.
(usage) 'I'll tell ye, Mary, it was so small he had a reddner.'

Ride (n)(v)

(*See also* shag)

An attractive female or male. (v) To partake in sexual intercourse.
(usage) 'I had a ride of that ride in Accounts.'

Scanger (n)

(*see also* Scrubber, Slapper)

Female lacking in sophistication.
(usage) 'The scanger drank her finger bowl.'

Scarlet (adj)

(see *also* Mortified)

Embarrassed. Blushing.

(usage) 'I was scarlet when I found out afterwards that he was a bishop.'

Scratcher (n)

Bed.

(usage) 'If you're not out of the scratcher and here in ten minutes operating on this man's brain, you're fired.'

Scrubber (n)

(see *also* Scanger, Slapper)

Woman of low moral fibre and little sophistication.

(usage) 'She's such a scrubber that she smokes during oral sex.'

Scutters (n)

Diarrhoea.
(usage) 'Eight pints of Harp and a curry always gives my missus the scutters.'

Shag (v)

(*see also* Ride)

To have sexual intercourse.
(usage) 'That Viagra is great shaggin' stuff.'

Shattered (adj)

Very tired. Requiring sleep.
(usage) 'Listen, Taoiseach. The whole Cabinet's been working for nearly an hour and we're all shattered.'

Shenanigans (n)

Mischievous, suspicious, underhand, devious goings-on.
(usage) 'Next item on today's County Council agenda: planning shenanigans. Sorry, uh, planning submissions.'

Shite (adj)

Of extraordinarily poor quality.
(usage) 'The health service is shite.'

Shite hawk (n)

Swine. Pig. Scumbag.
(usage) 'When I asked that shite hawk Sean what we'd use for protection he said we could use de bus shelter.'

Shower of savages

(expression)

Loud, ignorant, unsophisticated crowd of people.
(usage) Q: 'Who's that shower of savages in the corner?'
A: 'That's the Cabinet.'

Single (n)

Bag of chips.
(usage) 'Micko was so good in bed I nearly dropped me single.'

Skiver (n)

Person who avoids honest work.
(usage) Kid: 'When I grow up I want to be a skiver like you, Dad.'
Dad: 'So you want to work in the insurance industry, then?'

Slag (v)

Make fun of a person in a lighthearted, friendly manner.
(eg) 'Yer a big ignorant sleeven of a muck savage, ye thick bogtrotter ye.'

Slapper (n)

Female of low morals and poor taste in clothing.
(usage) 'You're not really going to make that slapper a Minister, are you, Taoiseach?'

Slash (n) (v)

Urination.
(usage) ' ... if I may interrupt my learned friend, m'Lud, as I'm dying for a slash.'

Sleeveen (n)

Devious, sly, repulsive individual.

(eg) Any member of Ireland's car insurance industry.

Spondulicks (n)

Money.

(usage) 'Hee hee, gentlemen. Wait'll ye see the spondulicks our insurance company screwed out of Irish drivers last year.'

Suckin' diesel (now yer)

(expression)

Now you're talking! Now you're doing well!

(usage) 'Increase car insurance premiums by 20% for no reason? Now yer suckin' diesel, Mr Chief Executive!'

Thick (adj)

Extremely stupid.

(eg) The person who conceived RTE's 'Angelus' slot.

Throw shapes (v)

To swagger excessively.

To show off.

(usage) 'Will you stop throwing shapes at those slappers or we'll never get a bleedin' shag.'

Up the pole (expression)

With child. Pregnant.

(usage) 'Great news, Ma, I'm up de pole. I mean, eh, engaged.'

Wagon (n)

Unattractive female.
(usage) *'Better gimme another pint. She still looks like a wagon.'*

Wojus (adj)

Extremely poor quality.
(usage) 'The bus service, the health service, the train service, the telephone service and every other bleedin' government service in Ireland is wojus.'

Wrecked (adj)

Extremely tired.
Worn out.
(usage) Ex-Civil Servant : 'I'm wrecked doing this ... what d'ye call it?'
Private Employee: 'Work.'

Yard
(get up the) **(expression)**

Get lost!
(usage) 'So, you drank three quarters of it before you realised it was a bad pint? Get up the yard!'

Yer wan **(n)**

Female whose name escapes one. Nondescript individual.
(usage) 'Yer wan over there. Yeah, her. Me wife.'

You're wha? **(expression)**

Alleged method of proposing to one's sweetheart on Dublin's northside.
(usage) 'You're bleedin' wha?'

Yer man Colin Murphy in de picture is a wojus head-the-ball who's regularly paralytic from de gargle. He's a bit of a bowsie and he's always on de doss. His normal job is writin' ads but when he's not up to ninety with that, he likes to do a little nixer, like this. His English is ganky, which makes him de deadly choice to give dis a lash.

Considered by many to be an authority on Irish slang ever since he was a little gurrier, Donal O'Dea came to prominence when he became the first person to accurately differentiate between a scanger, a scrubber and slapper. He's been working in advertising for donkey's years and is believed by his colleagues to be a bit of a mentaller.

OUT THE BOOK OF IRISH SONGS YER OU
OOLEY THE FECKIN' BOOK OF IRISH SEX
THE BOOK OF LUVELY IRISH RECIPES YE
ER THE FECKIN' BOOK OF IRISH SAYING
ER OF SAVAGES THE 2ND FECKIN' BOOK
RST ONE THE FECKIN' BOOK OF IRISH INS
HALF AS USEFUL THE BOOK OF FECKIN
S AND BOWSIES THE BOOK OF DEADLY IN
ALWAYS BLATHERIN' ON ABOUT THE B
WHEN HE WAS JARRED AT A HOOLEY THE
R DACENT PEOPLE'S EYES THE BOOK O
YOU WERE A LITTLE GURRIER THE FECK
E BATTER WITH A SHOWER OF SAVAGES
S A HOLY SHOW OF THE FIRST ONE THE
CK AS MANURE AND ONLY HALF AS USE
CRAIC FOR CUTE HOORS AND BOWSIES
FECKER IN THE PUB IS ALWAYS BLATHE
ELLA ALWAYS SANG WHEN HE WAS JAR
LOVE THAT'S NOT FIT FOR DACENT PEOP
A USETA MAKE WHEN YOU WERE A LITTLE
HEN YOU GO ON THE BATTER WITH A SH
SLANG THAT MAKES A HOLY SHOW OF
'S FOR GOBDAWS AS THICK AS MANU